7/4 1974

To Dick
with Love
Mignon

The Greatest Is Love

The Greatest Is Love

St. Paul's Wonderful Words

About Faith, Hope and Love

Illustrated by Lois Jackson

HALLMARK EDITIONS

Printed in the United States of America.
Library of Congress Catalog Card Number: 75-131520.
Standard Book Number: 87529-163-5.

The Greatest Is Love

I may speak in tongues
of men or angels,
but if I am without love,
I am a sounding gong
or a clanging cymbal.

I may have the gift

of prophecy,

and know every hidden truth...

I may have faith

strong enough

to move mountains…

But if I have no love,

I am nothing.

I may dole out all I possess,

or even give my body

to be burnt,

but if I have no love,

I am none the better.

Love is patient…

Love is kind

and envies no one.

Love is never boastful,

nor conceited, nor rude;

...does not gloat

over other men's sins,

but delights in the truth.

There is nothing

love cannot face...

There is no limit

to its faith,

its hope,

and its endurance.

Love will never come

to an end.

Are there prophets?

Their work will be over.

Are there tongues of ecstasy?

They will cease...

For our knowledge and

our prophecy alike

are partial

and the partial vanishes

when wholeness comes.

When I was a child,

my speech, my outlook,

and my thoughts

were all childish.

When I grew up,
I had finished
with childish things.

Now we see only puzzling
reflections in a mirror,
but then we shall see
face to face.

My knowledge now is partial;
then it will be whole,
like God's knowledge of me.

In a word, there are
three things
that last forever:
faith, hope, and love...

But the greatest of them all

is love.

Love